I0817517

TRANSIT

ALSO BY DAVID BAKER

POETRY

Whale Fall (2022)

Swift: New and Selected Poems (2019)

Scavenger Loop (2015)

Omul Alchimic (*Alchemical Man*, 2009, Romania, translated by Chris Tanasescu)

Never-Ending Birds (2009)

Treatise on Touch: Selected Poems (2007, UK)

Midwest Eclogue (2005)

Changeable Thunder (2001)

The Truth about Small Towns (1998)

After the Reunion (1994)

Sweet Home, Saturday Night (1991)

Haunts (1985)

Laws of the Land (1981)

PROSE

Show Me Your Environment: Essays on Poetry, Poets, and Poems (2014)

Talk Poetry: Poems and Interviews with Nine American Poets (2012)

Heresy and the Ideal: On Contemporary Poetry (2000)

EDITED BY

Collected Poems of Stanley Plumly (with Michael Collier, 2025)

Seek After: On Seven Modern Lyric Poets (2018)

Radiant Lyre: Essays on Lyric Poetry (with Ann Townsend, 2007)

Meter in English: A Critical Engagement (1996)

TRANSIT

POEMS

David Baker

W. W. NORTON & COMPANY
Independent Publishers Since 1923

Printed in the United States of America
First Edition

For information about special discounts for bulk purchases, please contact W. W. Norton Special Sales at specialsales@wwnorton.com or 800-233-4830

Manufacturing by Versa Press
Book design by Chris Welch
Production manager: Ramona Wilkes

ISBN: 978-1-324-11747-6

W. W. Norton & Company, Inc.
500 Fifth Avenue, New York, NY 10110
www.wwnorton.com

W. W. Norton & Company Ltd.
15 Carlisle Street, London W1D 3BS

1 2 3 4 5 6 7 8 9 0

for Page

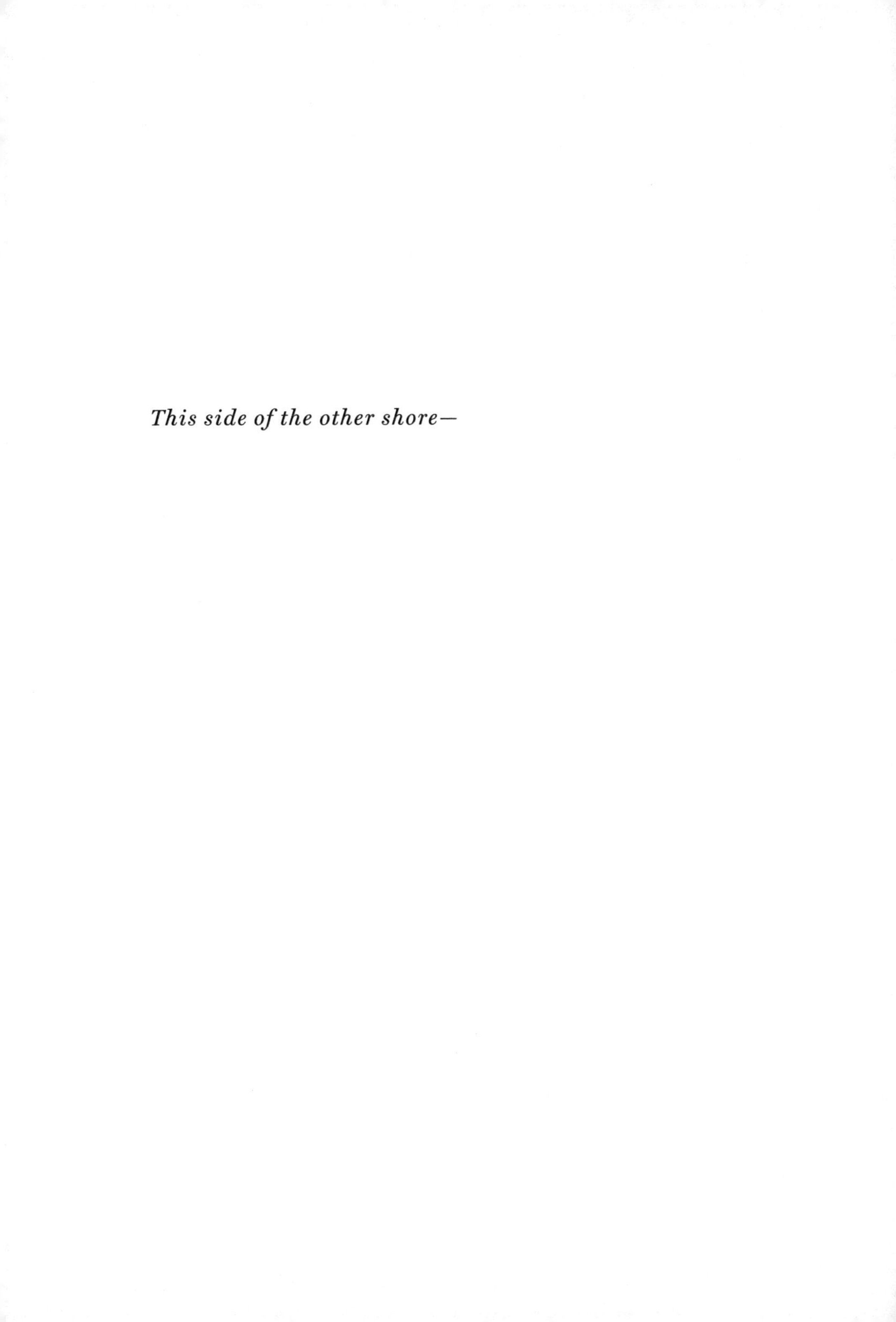

This side of the other shore—

ORDER OF POEMS

ONE

TWO

THREE

FOUR

FIVE

ONE

Six Notes

Come down to us. Come down with your song,
little wren. The world is in pieces.

We must not say so. In the dark hours,
in the nearest branches, I hear you thrum—

. . .

The deer come to die beside the creek.
Mud the color of walnut stain. Reek and

runoff from the new development, there,
beyond the woods. Rib and skull. No jawbone—

. . .

It makes a soundless scream. I hope for peace
when I walk here sometimes in the dark.

If not peace, clarity. If not clarity,
at least a place to breathe. Else I'll scream, too—

. . .

Come down, little dove, far above the bay.
I hear you in a thirsty palm or up

beyond the rocks. A windy reed of song.
Blue sun, blue cloud above the sweeping bay—

. . .

Sometimes we have to say so. I don't know how.
A man, a boy, an anger with no tongue

took his automatic rifle to school today.
The report we hear, discharge, echo—

. . .

is the sound of sorrow, reloading.
No matter where we walk, we hear it call.

Little wing, little creek, little bay, dark hour.
Come down with your beaks of morning and blood—

Late Georgic in a Field in Ohio

Take my hand, she said, and I lay my palm on top of her hand and she knelt a little, I knelt beside her, and she waved gently, as with a wand, the small light she held like a pencil, tracing in the humming air a phosphorescent *J*. We were in clover, we were in jimson, in the field, we were in sedge grasses wet with the birthing of mid-evening. I have been a biologist all my life, she said, and I love this more than anything. *J* in the deep blue air, *J J* and the redwing blackbirds chipped from the cattails around the pond and a jet glided homebound or outbound in the low horizon. *J* she wrote, we wrote, and then a blink answered from its cave of curled grasses and another came toward us in a funny sort of dancing rise-and-fall, and I realized we were speaking, all of us, firefly and awkward human couple-not-a-couple, and the wonder was not that they answered us. The wonder was it dawned on us finally to ask.

Jewelweed,

touch-me-not, or in the taxonomic
registry *Impatiens capensis*, can

be orange or spotted. Can be *pallida,*
in its yellow slightly larger version—

. . .

You're kidding. Nope. Dunk two leaves in the creek,
where it runs down cold, and you get emeralds

in your palm. I mean it. Rub the sap
where the ivy bit you—and you won't itch—

. . .

The flowers have tubal "elongations."
Nectar "spurs." Bumblebees love them. Ruby-

throats love them. Pollination's "very high,"
says the book. What accounts for such a name?—

. . .

There's two or three in the scrub-line along
the fencerow, right there, next to the ivy.

Looks like the inner ear bones of a wolf.
Like you've seen *those*. Well, pictures. It's close—

. . .

Don't touch that. I mean it. It's called
poison for a reason. When I was a kid

I helped my dad clear this field. I breathed in
smoke from our big brush fire, and ended up—

. . .

in the ICU. Like you've seen wolf bones.
It's called a doctrine of signatures.

What a thing looks like should give you its name.
Where a thing grows, its other will be nigh—

. . .

Come on, that's too much, who says nigh.
Get back. I'm looking to see if it smells.

There's a couple more leaning there—"poppers"—
the way the little seeds bust out. Whistle-weed—

. . .

Toothwort. Eyebright. Little orange balsam.
Galen said things will grow beside the thing

they remedy, waiting right there for you.
They tell you what they are. Galen's the wolf?—

. . .

I don't know why I come out here with you.
Sure you do. Listen, there's a whippoorwill.

That's a lonesome sound. Well, there's two of them.
You think it's going to rain? Smells like rain—

Can You Say It

1.

There was a busyness. Yes, in the apple tree.
The first light. You could say it was a busyness—
like a hive of movements, indistinct as haze

caught up in strings of light. Low sunlight, among webs.
And along the strands those slender brown fingerlings,
the leaves, hovered, just there, in the breeze.

2.

What I meant to say is the morning was heavy.
Was it our sorrow. The tree was at the window.
Before we could see the webs, the dew, the thousand

little apples, we saw the end of it only. The night, yes—
the end of it. There is always something else to say.
No, I mean the first light. There's far too much to say.

3.

Low sunlight. Yes, in the apple tree, coming up.
Every day is the anniversary of a terror.
But there you are. A sorrow. And something

caught there dazzling in the haze, just the same. Yes.
And of this moment closer to you than I can say.
There was busyness in the apple tree.

4.

First I thought it just a slim leaf, hanging
        to the screen. On the door. The night was settled.
        Darkness inside, darkness out. Then the wings

half-closed like hands, or a clasp. I mean, of a jewel.
        Dust of a moth, half-a-palm wide, and the crickets
        a busy tide at the seashore, when this was a sea.

5.

In the morning, the moth was gone. Or was it silence.
        Every day the image at the window—us, each other,
        wings on the door. Yes, can you say it now.

Before the webs we saw first light, a breath of haze—
        then leaves, floating there. In the window, yes. We saw
        ourselves. Then we saw ourselves with shadows.

Twilight Sleep

I walked down to the water. Trees were there. Birds were.
Low sky tipped in the sandbar willow. Gray as a slurry—

My love heard sawing. Was it music? Well, she could walk.
It was slow, like Keith at Köln. Then not, for the pain—

Creeks cut through. Whippoorwills. All the calling swallows.
And limestone ledges, boulders big as trucks, as cabins—

The house was there. Ruined and fallen and nowhere
to be seen, now, but a gentle hump in the hillside—

. . .

My love smelled river. Roses. *Must there be complications.*
Surgical stainless, since you asked, and a Tufnol peen—

I walked down to the water. Metaphyseal fit with rotational
fixation is key to survivorship. *I wasn't sure I was awake*—

Like hovering ghosts, in their gowns. The twilight sleep.
All the little stars through the leaves it was chilly not cold—

Old bottles, china shards, standing chimney of river rock.
We marked our way by the willow with the scar 10 feet up—

. . .

I walked down to the water. Dad picked me up—sixty years by.
Carried me over the river over stones over moon-glister there—

Microscopic sections show eburnation and subchondral sclerosis.
Synovium—*if you really wanna know*—pseudocyst formation—

And him with his hand, swollen as a ball glove—catfish
no bigger than a twig stuck in our seine. Spike *got me good*—

What I want to say is, in the shadows, in the twilight,
in the solitary place, the heart lies open to the world—

. . .

Two steps. Be careful. She is learning to walk again.
Across the room. *Once you take three then you've got it*—

Around the block, the park. The *Valley News* noted
the gray-haired woman *marching along, hair in a bun*—

Miles a day. Catfish envenomation. Cutaneous edema.
Severe necrosis. Death has been reported, says the report—

My love walked down to the water, salt urn in her arms.
Doves on the bridge-beams. Taking the daughter's path—

. . .

Well, Doc's the best. He likes music in his sterile room.
You mean cicatrix? You mean ghost limb? Was it a storm?—

We hack it off and whack the new piece—light titanium—
with a hammer. It snugs the hollow. Papillary w/mild fibrosis—

We pulled the seine with two willow saplings. Crawdads.
Minnows. We walked down to the water. *Put your hand in*—

We were ankle-deep in the creek, in tennis shoes.
It was warm, like crickets. Slipping on mussels on moss—

. . .

Years don’t matter. The heart lies open to the world.
Willow scar six feet up. Trees were there. Birds were—

It’s how you know where you are. My love walked down
to the water, carrying ash. Walked back with her scars—

So we lean together, over the ancient waters. Big sky
like music. All the night, freckled with doves with stars—

Listening to songs to be sung on the other side. Of what?
We will stay a while, by the water, until we are water—

TWO

Field Notes by a Slender Path

I held a bird
in my hand. No.

It was a game—
a child's game. No,

my bird friend said
when he unstrung

the mist net where
one bird hung mid-

flight, between scrub
and sumac, by

the slender path.
Like this. He placed

it so. In my
open palm—then

closed my fingers
fingers-up. Female

yellow warbler
he said, and he

barely turned her
leg to read the

band there, while I—
how can I say

this—felt our hearts
in one gray breath.

Edge juvenile.
In the game, as

hard as you can,
you clap your hands.

Clench one fist—
throttle your wrist.

Maybe your friend
presses your thumb,

so that it stings,
goes numb, goes ash.

The net is blowing.
It's delicate

as a soft cloud.
You count to ten.

Now loosen—one
by one, your fingers . . .

you know the rest.

Lilac Tree and Lichen

1.

How little time. The fevers were worst then.
Early evenings. As the air cooled. As breezes,
barely there, pressed down through the tree.

We had no good words for it—the scent of the tree—
not quite roses, nor a clean sea air, but more
the flavor of some happiness, when we were happy.

2.

I could taste it in the corners of my mouth.
My fevers. Like green-white tips of flowers
on our tree, each cluster of foam, each panicle

a palmful. For a year the doctors couldn't say
what to call it. It was my illness. Named by
symptoms only, my fever-few, my blackthorn.

3.

We called it our fringe tree—no. Japanese lilac,
our tree friend would tell us. *Syringa reticulata*.
The only species grown to such heights. And no,

it's not lichen but a lichen-likely fungi.
You probably won't die—not of this. Soft laughter.
Like light from a candle. In clusters, in evening,

4.

the green stem-like branchings. Like coral.
Sometimes I was so empty I could listen to
the heartbeat of breezes, there, among trees.

Then years. How uncertain the words. We laughed
a little together, and each time we spoke of the tree—well,
what else have we got wrong is what we meant.

The Middle Voice

A white bird was taken. Was it a bird.
Wisps of feathers, long, hair-thin in a breeze
along the pathway, along the stones there.
Yes, above the shore. The bird was a flower.
Your hand made a shadow the better to see.
Berries rimmed the slender twigs there.
Caper berries the book said later when
we looked. *Cynophalla flexuosa*,
if it matters. Did it fly. Doves were
calling from wires and the lime trees
all the way to the waters beyond which rain
was coming down from small clouds. White
petals. Hot stone scent of it. Sun-on-stone,
but the rain midway from the clouds.
Was it rain. The rain was taken before
it was down. My hand in yours. When
you see one you see the many more
quivering in green nests of the shrubs.
They are whole wings they are so delicate.
You can't feel them like the rain not
falling on your face though you breathe it.
The clouds passed. One stayed in place.

Childhood

I miss the cold, but not the cold breaking,
not the small limbs sheared, nor the icepick cold
white wind working its whole way through you
no matter your coat and gloves, and no matter
the blue scarf someone tied and tucked tight.

The same cold blue all day in the sky. Frozen
blue through limbs of the two standing elms.
Brilliant each blue. Blue the color of new
snow like wafers on the fields. Come in cold then,
and the dark comes with you, kick off your boots

and someone is rubbing your feet so they
sting, then stop stinging. Now the bruised apple-
red bottle at the foot of your bed, steaming,
and come morning woodsmoke in the kitchen.
I miss the cold then, so cold there is singing.

Small Weathers

The first of dawn. The silver rain from hours ago
still tipping off the lowest leaves—

and along the sky's edge at the grass line, a pink light
foxing now, running to new shadows—

                                                            amplitude,
discarding beauty and death as unequal to the moment—

With sandpaper and caulk we'd worked the bad wall.
A putty knife, then smaller, a Q-tip—

                                                                                                    but not until
she put a finger to it, smoothing there, daubing,
was our work right. An invisible finish.

—but whorls of her fingerprint, where she'd touched me,

and *the tree of veins trembles*—

Inside, outside. The wind, the little waters, coating
the thin fabric of each blade shining there.

Is it the wind that shakes inside me, too?
I should know. Weeks or a day. Watching the quiver

in my hands.
Wind where the chimes will be

Beautiful in a passing way—

All those years I couldn't tell sorrow from sleeplessness.
Pain from illness . . .

Listen. Now it's 3 a.m.
and someone thinks enough of this life

to sing, out there, in the far field, a few minutes more. Listen,

a little longer.
—the birds starting to sleep, their songs
becoming silent, then their silence—

This morning in the city the huff of a bus,
couriers on motor bikes and now, tonight,

at home in the quiet village of stars, the wordless
vespers of a far catbird—

                                        magnitude, he said at
the end, for which *we should give thanks*—

THREE

My Documentary Art

1.

Then I stepped into
        the woods, over the rusted teeth.
Out of the tansy meadow,
        among thistle there, the green milkweed.
I crossed into the woods.
        Cooler there, air of the shadows.
Low breeze and the leaves.
        Darker there under pawpaws between
the fence and little
        creek. No longer mine
—not for years—though my shadow
        led me through shadows
to where I learned
        how to wait. May apples, their soft fists
unfurling, brown ginger, jack-
        in-the-pulpit along the old path.

2.

Tell me. Who owns a tree.
        Who owns a stone.
A step. My friend Phil says
        the document extends the art.
He's walking through
        his own tangle of thoughts—ten years past—
talking to himself.
        Ephemeral now the coltsfoot, the yellow
trout lily in the thicket.
        Full disclosure—Phil's quoting Rukeyser.

He says, in turn,
    the art extends the document. When
I first flattened the plat
    with my hand to the table,
the better to read alongside
    the deed, I counted each contour line—

3.

down to the circle pasture,
    from the top of the ravine—so when
I walked there
    I'd know, written in scrub,
the slope. Meadowlarks this time,
    or—I still can't tell
which—maybe swallows, are
    kettling above
the big tulip tree by the creek.
    I haven't spoken one word, in three days,
to a single person
    in person.
I wanted, at least,
    to get it in writing, while I could.
The little spread of them.
    Just there, the first time, in the grit and shadow

4.

—wild ramps, I mean—
        past the tulip. I stepped over the fence.
I'd come for
        no good reason, except to be
lost there, and alone.
        Maybe you know what I mean.
Found them in humus
        around the deadfall oak, below the shade sides
of pine and chestnut trunks
        mossy with their own old news.
So I wrote it all—here—
        *twenty steps—past ramps—*through the little bell-
white flowers of May apples, through
        a scatter of all the
ephemerals. They'd popped up
        —the morels, I mean—

5.

more shadow
        at first than mushroom. Phil says
each investigation . . . *extends*
        the very idea of what poetry is and what it can do.
The more I looked the
        more I found. And though I've been here
many times since,
        and found no more, I come often
down dusty roads,
        through someone else's fields, out of

tansies, out
        of canker weed and rust, for the shadows'
wild company. And for
        the quiet. It is nameless, and nowhere,
and without end. Tell me.
        Who owns that.

Six Glasses of Water

The creek's running down cold from the high hills.
We spend a good hour turning over stones.

Each one—a crawdad. Quick shiner. Slick moss.
A shadow, exposed. We count what's under.

. . .

Willow hangs its hair over the cool pools.
Roots hang there, too—knots—shimmery copies.

We float tennis balls down a hundred feet
to gauge the drop—rate of the down-flow—

. . .

where the riffles, the sand bars, where the slow
places go, how slow. When the governor

held his presser—two weeks after the de-
railed train spilled a toxic mess, three counties

. . .

over—he walked to a sink and filled
six glasses of bright water from the tap.

Neighbors have been scared. Children sickened.
Coughing. Is it asthma. Will it get worse—

. . .

No one's coming to help us. Pollution
plumes float beyond a burning. The high pines

stand out against the weird yellow sky.
Or do we imagine that. My friend Andy—

. . .

says farms. Dips a vial for trace pesticides.
The creek fidgets and spins off at an eddy.

We skim a quiet surface for algae.
For striders, seed husks, nothings like these—

. . .

The governor takes a sip. He takes two—

Mammalian

1.

Stubborn. That's one thing.
The little brown bat,
        whom scholars call *Myotis lucifugus*,

will not be moved to
leave its habitat,
        so is dying now in drastic numbers.

A culprit pathogen,
which causes white-
        nose syndrome, multiplies their "fungal load"

by spreading through the
bats' epidermal
        tissue during hibernation. To wit:

the virus *Pseudo-*
gymnoascus
        destructans—can you believe that?—traced

from Eurasia to
New York, through the Midwest,
        just since 2006. It's invasive

as kudzu or
capitalism. It
        infects the established hibernacula

of the little bats,
who won't abandon
        their nesting grounds. Such places the scholars

agree are "suboptimal habitat."

2.

Ours was high in a shadow of rafters.
My father swept it, lightly, with a towel
—1960-something—so I carried it
loose in a pillowcase to the basement,
to the aquarium we packed with twigs,
damp grass, a little pie-tin to drink from,
its long wings "very much like a human
arm and hand," its tan skin taut as suede pulled
across a fine branching of bone. All day

it would not eat. What could it see? Echo
and sorrow—I mean ours—though we tried eye-
droppers of egg, houseflies dropped in. We tried
to apologize with care. Delicate
tipped folds of its ears, mouse fur, but one wing
awry, like a twig snapped, useless. They lack,
said our book, "eyeshine," though little brown bats
can be distinguished by hairs on their feet
that extend beyond the length of their toes.

3.

Maybe memory
isn't a science
        but, like science, is a way of knowing.

The bats stay true to
their known refugia—
        problem is, per one study, they "continue

to select habitats
where *P. destructans*
        severity is highest." Such sites become,

scholars tell us,
"ecological traps."
        The data's undeniable: where pre-

and post-invasion
comparisons show
        a "distribution shift analysis . . .

a large proportion
[52%] still
        used relatively warm roosts." They won't, that

is, be moved—though
"fungal loads increase
        with early hibernation roosting

temperatures." The instinct to stay's too strong.

4.

The last I saw was last month, the last light
over the windward islands, like a wing.
We were in love again. We were in the glow
of stars alive or long dead. Suddenly
they were with us, skittering just above
our bay balcony. The bare wind with wings.
Sipping mosquitoes. Unmistakable
their flight lines, jagged as constellations.
Fruit or free-tailed, an island cousin, up

from their inward caves or scrub woods. Peepers
called then, and doves; a cargo ship passed
slowly out of sight. We apologized
for what we had done. Stubborn. I mean us.
And the other thing. There are so many
—bobcat and vole, killer whale, bonobo—
in the vast taxonomy of mammalia.
Yet these remain the only ones of us
able to
            —of course, this one never would—fly.

Oikos

1.

You better count
your blessings, huh—

that's what she said.
Where do I start.

She'd thumped me with
her SUV.

Backing out fast.
And down I went,

grocery sacks dropped,
jam jars shattered,

apples bouncing . . .
Well, my bad—then

whirr her window.

. . .

Where *does* one start. *First of all [get yourself] an* oikos—

He means, by *oikos*, a dwelling place, your hearth-and-home—

But stop right there. Hesiod's a jerk, right? He goes on—

To say, *[get yourself] a woman and a plower ox—*

A bought woman, not a wife, one who could follow the—

Oxen and get all goods into their right place in—

The oikos . . . It's rural Aeolis, it's early in—

The 7th century, BCE. Men own the goods—

The property, and to be sure, Hesiod can plant—

A hale field, furnish a dwelling. He can sketch out specs—

To build your new plow. Knows *there are a hundred timbers—*

To a wagon. He drafts it all—stock, tree, pole, tail—

For a *fitted plow*, and can instruct the best handling—

Of your team, *as they pull the yoke peg by the yoke strap—*

He gives, that is, a fine accounting for his business—

Plus, it's important to remember, what Hesiod—

Is most concerned about is getting enough to eat—

As Tandy and Neale put it. It's as simple as that—

2.

Simplicity,
simplicity,

simplicity!
So why did he

have to say it
three times? Thoreau

—surveyor, scrounge—
is Hesiod's true

heir. No doubt, though
Virgil's no slouch

either, grafting
orchards, sowing

fields . . . *so spring begins . . .*

. . .

So spring begins. I was going for supplies, for home—

My daughter coming back. Page flying in from New York—

Where do I start. More eggs, milk and bread, something to grill—

A treat, two treats. Apples. It's important to keep things—

Your beloveds will enjoy. Keep them welcome, safe, warm—

But Hesiod's advice is built on slavery, too—

With *bought women*, and strict adherence to the costs of things—

Thoreau's a tool, too—(no pun there)—fine-tuning his transit—

For a survey—stingy, proud of his profit-and-expense—

Coming up to the good by $8.71½—

For his *experience in raising beans*. At Walden—

When guests won't tend to things for themselves, he coins the term—

Hospitalality, and hopes they'll get the hint and—

Leave. *Oikos*. Just look at the etymology there—

It's the root from which ecology stems, but also—

Economy, a getting-and-spending of our earth—

(Why are givers of advice so often misanthropes?—

So often misers? Misogynists? Or is it just me?)—

3.

Anyway, I
went for a walk.

Down the six blocks.
Through the village.

Past the great oaks.
I had my list.

I took my time—
waving in turn

to my neighbors.
How does he [sic]

live, I wonder?
You know the rest—

my brush with death.
Okay, dust-up

in the car lot—

. . .

I would like to leave a good accounting of my life—

And leave, when I leave, by a quiet path. I have grown—

Beans (many), cardoons, rhubarb, beets, tomatoes (many)—

But with less sun at my new house, now, my smaller yard—

I'm content with ferns and flowering shrubs, trees (many)—

Herbs (sage, parsley, lavender), under one crab apple—

I recycle and reuse. I waste and want. I know—

I've sponsored a thousand terrors. Damages. Deep harm—

For, as Virgil says, *life brings sickness with it.* I've hoped—

To make, at least, my artful *oikos.* Or let's call it—

Such business, on our earth, that the beloveds may know—

I left word for them, in these rough songs, to ease their lives—

The days are longer now. It's cold out. I worry I'll—

Be left, *clutching at shadows, with still so much to say*—

Where do I begin? It's not that hard. Brush myself off—

Gather my things, to start back for home. They'll be coming—

Soon. *Flute music high in the beech leaves.* So on we go—

Six Meditations on a Poem

I'm walking across the shiny black asphalt of our local grocery parking lot. It's 7 a.m., straight up and down, and there are only a couple of cars, one pickup, no one else around. The store opens at 7 and I'm out of milk. It's also the end of May. The morning air hangs already humid, very still, yet several dozen of the seeds I love come floating—down, sideways, even back upward—out from the trees, out of the gray-blue sky, across the parking lot. They mark the season as well as any calendar. It's the cottonwoods. They grow here in the village, down along Raccoon Creek, running alongside the grocery store; they grow through the low wetlands in and out of town and far beyond. Now you are—

Crossing against traffic, an otherwise.
Or the barest new breeze, slipping over
the white barn,
                    itself a conditional—

Speak what they will—

The cottonwood tree grows tall and can reach 100 feet in maturity. Its eastern variety (*Populus deltoides*) is common across eastern North America and southeastern Canada. Its bark is silver-white and relatively smooth, though as they age the trees turn more fissured, darkening with the years. I love their big leaves, relatively late to come on and early in autumn to fall, and especially I love the magic of their catkin flowers that release seed-capsules (samaras) to split open, broadcasting all these tiny cottony billows, silky white, and seemingly weightless. One tree, according to my tree book, can produce 40 million seeds in a single season.

Is it a barn. Is it white. Either way
you pause, in a stillness, and the quick
thermal stalls.
                    But on they come, floating—

they are but wind—

I've been reading Anne Bradstreet again, the steady sanity of her poems, the balance of her language and form, the clarity of her tender but righteous worldview. Cottonwoods would have been plentiful in her Massachusetts villages, in Cambridge, Ipswich, and her eventual residence in Andover. I bet she'd have called the cottonwoods "stately," though I find no reference to the species in her writings. But she did refer to tall elms and oaks alike as "stately." In "Contemplations" she meditated on trees, on "goodly" rivers and "gliding streams," often drawn to these landscapes for the serenity and privacy they provided for her.

With their hundred hair-fine small fires.
Their bright filaments. Is this the city.
Each doorway, an exit,
                                        a lit exhaustion—

In grass, on trees, in flight—

Mistress Bradstreet liked to walk. So do I. Roger Gilbert has a wonderful book, *Walks in the World*, about poetry, about poets walking, and the physical and meditative effect of just going on a walk. Wallace Stevens's poem "An Ordinary Evening in New Haven," Wordsworth's masterpiece *The Prelude*, and so many more lyric poems take the occasion of the walk as a time to think and sing. Gilbert offers a typological sorting even the Puritans might appreciate. He says there are three distinct transformational effects that modern poets attain through the habit of walking: the cognitive, the meditation, and the aesthetic.

Where a soul weighs less than the word for it.
Between her last touch, the wings of it,
and a next stitch of breeze.
                                        They fill the air—

Some fall down. Some fly up—

Let's say "Now You Are" can be simply a poem about walking and spring—the week or two when milkweed silks fill the air, whether you're in the city or the country, whether there is a wind or stillness. Let's imagine Anne Bradstreet alongside me on this walk, and we talk a bit, and she adds a phrase or two between my stanzas. My ghost companion. The italic fragments are from her poem "The Four Elements" and her letter "For My Dear Son Simon Bradstreet." I'm looking for all kinds of crossings-over—the street, the seeds across in the air, our crosstalk, the centuries touching and dissolving. "The Four Elements" is beautiful for its passages on air and wind and on water. Her elegant, rhymed couplets may be a ghost inside my poem, and her habit of reading large, divine purposes into every single tiny natural thing plays across the background. I see all these floating cottonwood seeds as words, too, or Bradstreet's angels, bits of a soul, glimpses of the many worlds.

And illuminate the air. Like a trembling
of waters where cottonwoods grow tall.
The cilia, the silk of them.
                                        Nothing's moving—

which may reveal a mind—

I think we live in many times at once. We live in many places at once. Our words are hardly ours, so much as the gifts and intimations of all their previous uses. The meditative walk of my poem is looking for ways to find forms and voices of the plural, the ongoing, the here-and-now and just-beyond. Can a poem—fixed on the two-dimensional plane of a page—suggest a third or even further dimensions? Can a word or a phrase find its usages in more than a single sentence, in more than one person's voice? What are those magical silky seeds but answers of "yes" to the questions? They are ghosts, gifts, whispers, defying gravity, place, and time.

When everything's on the move. Your soul is
not just for other worlds—it's for this one.
Like *something I leave*

for you in writing.

F O U R

Pocket Garden in the City

You would miss it if you were hurrying.
If you were harried or the day was drab.

It's tucked between two old brownstones, now
a defunct pet store, a popup for sneakers.

Take the stone path back. It's so narrow—
the leaning greenery like sticky sleeves,

sunflower above, like a lighthouse, the ocean
aroma of yellow hibiscus. But what are they doing.

Two cops, in the back corner, under a tropical lime.
Hooded figure between them—what's your name.

You stand there and they stand there.
Snapdragon. Hollyhock. Day lilies ablaze.

The Colonists

1.

Basalt the stone. Pillow igneous. Limestone, upthrust
in radiolarian chert and eroded into clasts,
out of the sea—

90 million years, give or take, ago. The ancient Turonian,
or second phase, of the Cretaceous. And what
have we here—

. . .

Ooh, I would *wear* that, a friend Tweets back
when I post the video. The worm is six inches long,
it's pulling—

itself by orange prolegs up a frangipani trunk.
Come look. Red bulb head, a coral-with-gray-
specked collar—

. . .

Burnished pitch its thorax and banded lime between
eight body-chambers. It's poisonous—but let's
not tell—since the—

host the frangipani has poison latex compounds, too.
Our stone driveway running down from the house
                                                            above the bay—

2.

Is lined with these. Also palms, dogbane, gardenia.
It's taken so long to get here. And if you step
                                                            off the main road—

far across the island, down a little bank, there's
another road. Remnant of the Old Danish Way.
                                                            It's cobblestone—

. . .

Maybe six paces wide, a hundred feet of it
remaining, give or take, suddenly out of the
                                                            boulders and scrub—

of the 18th century. *Time likewise does not exist by itself,*
but a sense follows from things themselves . . .
                                                            (Lucretius)—

. . .

As out of the sea, the rock land. Out of rock, the road
cut by hand into rough cobbles for
                                        the cane wagons—

donkey teams. People roped and lined up behind. People
—Jesus Christ—on the miserable road, manor to mill
                                        to slave quarters—

3.

Shadowed still in torchlight. Kiln smoke
curls through the mangrove limbs, above salt ponds.
                                        Acrid smell—

of *what has been done in the past*, what now is present . . .
Around the millstone a footpath for turning
                                        200 gallons of—

. . .

Sugarcane water a day. *Dick, 25, able field negro, £140* . . .
Daub walls, thatch-cane the roofs, the rain.
                                        Now we're here—

on vacation. We've ordered a la carte. We walk the ankle-
turning cobbles matted with blade cactus and sea sedge,
                                        and cool our—

. . .

Drinks with ice from the fridge. Beside the house
the same massive ledge of stone, older than animals.
A bat cuts over—

our deck light. Shh says the sea. Let's take a walk,
you say, by the frangipani again. What would you like
with your tea.

Says the Wind

She's got her eyes down.
                                                  He's got his head down
as far as he can pull it into his scarf and burly coat.

Their shoulders are pitched forward hard to cut
through the city headwind. But there is no wind—

. . .

What we see of a wind is what we see
of the world of things. Not wind but a chaff

of pollen choking in that whirl. Muster of leaves
above in the puffed-out ash. What she says—

. . .

What we cannot hear but see on each face.
Now he's walking ahead. Now he's lost

in a fluster of subway riders shoving up
out of the sudden portal. Shh says the wind—

. . .

The soul of another lies in darkness.
Now she is running and now she is calling

into the choppy pool of people. Everyone
shoves into this wind. But there is no wind—

The Other Sorrow

1.

Before the fallen the falling. The night the snow the evening shifting—

Before the faint snow floating in the air—the sleepwalkers—

The little basket of sorrows. Before this, more snow on top—

Of old crabapple leaves gathering there for months   the months—

Before the piles in the dark corners   the dark corners. Before—

The falling, forty-five minutes each flake—the sidle-and-drift—

Before the many things not said here   among the never-to-be—

Fallen—each shifting—each not-fallen not-said thing   not said—

Before my frail my basket   what the future has already forgotten—

2.

Why so sad? To which the other turned toward the lake—

Blue glaze-like sky, cobalt with sun seams. Like ceramic—

Lately thrown. That's not it. Wind in the miniature crab—

The thousand tiny apples   scrubbed with first dew. Shaking—

And dripping   each the size of a wren's heart. That's—

Not it. No after it has sung—in alarm—trying to attract—

Flown now into another yard, another tree. What do you—

Mean. *Sorrow is unsafe when it is real sorrow.* Hear them—

Singing? They are gone. You can still hear them singing—

Island Birds

Come twilight, come the hue of shadows,
she's there on the cable just beyond our deck.
She's watching, you tell me, she knows we're back.
We've come for two weeks to write, and rewrite . . .
But now she coos. Makes that lowing sound
her kind is known for. Sometimes she stays quiet.
Small red eyes, dust-yellow ring around each,
a pale rust to her shoulders. Scaly-necked dove.
There's nothing reptilian about her but her name.

—And not to be confused with the bigger anis,
with their black-ridged bills, mostly back in the trees.
Or the sleek, arrow-shot bananaquit, its
high overtones of song as it skips tree to
bush to beyond the brown curve of the bay.
And not of course the incessant, exploratory,
omnipresent thrashers. Pearly-eyed, says our book.
One's prone to hopping along the handrail, staring in
where we sit with our grievances and pet names.

—But now the white smudge of a shower.
Far clouds. A hammering in the hills above.
But that scent. Is it more hibiscus than lime?
What are we to do with a world so lovely?
You want a name for our trouble, too.
I'm better with birds, and that's my trouble.
Yours is to ask me again. What shall we
call the troubling thing we share? Give me a name.
—This world flown into the hands of our kind.

FIVE

Watchers

The barely tufted one. The gray small silent one.
The yellow-stripe-above-the-red-wing-striped one
in her black cardigan, though the day's still hot—
the little that's left of day and the hazy high sky.

The one alone, two to the side. Shoulders aligned.
Then in minutes the dozen more pulling up
so quiet in golf carts we hear a soft munching
of gravel and one or two gulls flapping then

lifting from lamps flickering along the lake walk.
They're tightly nosed-in in a row, like drive-ins
they remember, and the sun drifts lower still
beyond the boathouse in a long dazzle of

lake shimmering yellow softer toward gold.
They're facing it all, beneath tall lindens,
like a breakwater for the village behind them.
It's not far away. They are ready to go.

After Long Illness

So one day I
went for a walk.

Walked down to the
kingfisher creek.

It had been five
years, maybe more—

down I counted
the many steps

past the wood duck
ponds. Mid-April.

The spring peepers
sang—*Pseudacris*

crucifer cru-
cifer—from moss

logs and willow
mulch, from cattails

low and high all
around these trees.

Their brown song rose
and fell in little

gasps. Sycamore.
Sassafras. While

a goldfinch pulled
a slender thread

from height to height.
There is no more

story to tell—
except I had

not died. And
one sound I heard,

along the small
wing of creek, I

still cannot name.
I seldom speak

of such things, though
I had come so

far to hear it.
Was it my soul?

What do I know?
The sound the wind

made, deep in those
trees. Cottonwood.

Birch. And the leaves
utterly still.

The Bay

How many stories among the stars.
The boats come in. The boats go out.

Our friend is dying. He writes,
he says, more often. Yet more sparely.

Now to see what wasn't seen before.

. . .

We stay up all night again to scan
the sky from our deck above the bay.

How slow the constellations spin.
Invincible heroes. Unrequited loves—

until, it seems, we've lost all count.

. . .

Soon we'll go, too. *Star, therefore, to start.*
A cargo freighter pulls across the waters.

We can tell from the placement of the lights,
the slow procession of it all. And so it's dawn.

Did I say invincible? I mean invisible.

Sense of

When, only later, the tawny owl called
(is it a night hawk? is it hunting, what does
it want? or the cry of an animal not above
but beyond us, through the tree line,
from the long field we'd walked that morning)—

It takes no time to lose the sense of things.

What I mean to say is, only later, we consulted
the book of answers. We knew what we had
heard, only then, the source of a hunger
out of which the call came, and the other
we did not hear, who had no need, to be heard—

Sailing Stones

Then here we are, scrabbling the dry creek. Bob stands up.
I stand up—breeze in the willows

and whippoorwill song, sweeping the rock ridges.
This was years ago.

This was yesterday. Trilobite in a shale plate. A tube of coral,
or a slim leaf-stem—

. . .

One eye's a weeper. One's settled—if I stay in the shadows.
Both doctors say

implants will shift. Acuity comes, but slowly.
This shouldn't be here—

. . .

What?
Bob's got another rock in his hands. It's chipped,
like an old bowling ball.

Black basalt. Errant—down from Canada, I'd say.
Pre-Cambrian. Come

a long way from home, and dropped in the melt. Yep,
in the last glaciation—

. . .

A million slivers of sunlight sheer off in the pines.
Star-burst floaters, jay-caws,

the scent of old water, and stones. I feel like I've been here
a billion billion years—

. . .

Bob's moving closer now, up the creek, tapping
his rock-hammer

—*Whoa Nellie!*—and grinning. *Where'd you get your math?*
This was yesterday.

And a hundred trillion neutrinos, in one second, pass
through your hand—

. . .

I've read it. Everything loose is traveling.
I always wonder

why you keep coming back here. It's not yours
anymore, am I right?—

. . .

Sometimes I see myself as part of the endless tide
—trees, or eons, or star-swirl—

if you look far enough and slow. The sailing stones
of Death Valley, Bob told me

—this was years ago—buoyant as paper cups in a stream,
but you can't see them moving—

. . .

etch long paths, *without animal intervention,*
across the sandflats. As though

on an ice sheet. *An ephemeral winter pond.*
I can see it now—

. . .

floating away from my beloveds, my friends,
                    the drift farther

from everyone, farther alone. It's what I wouldn't
                    have wanted. What I am.

I let my eyes go blur. White wings, white clouds.
                    And now we're moving, along the creek bed—

. . .

the shale plates, endless currents and spinning matter,
                    and immeasurable, empty time.

We've picked enough for today, don't you think?
                    Shadows of trees longer than the trees—

. . .

This was yesterday. This was years ago.
                    We've got our bags of ancients,

and now Bob's rinsed off and nestled his rock
                    in the backseat of my truck.

Soon we'll be ten miles down the road,
                    then farther, toward the sea—

ACKNOWLEDGMENTS

These poems first appeared in the following periodicals, to whose editors I extend my grateful acknowledgment: *The American Poetry Review*, "The Colonists," "Field Notes by a Slender Path"; *The Atlantic*, "Says the Wind"; *Bennington Review*, "My Documentary Art"; *The Georgia Review*, "Sailing Stones"; *The Hopkins Review*, "The Other Sorrow (1)"; *Image*, "After Long Illness," "The Other Sorrow (2)"; *New England Review*, "Late Georgic in a Field in Ohio," "Lilac Tree and Lichen"; *The New Yorker*, "The Bay," "Can You Say It," "Childhood," "Pocket Garden in the City," "Six Notes"; *Poetry*, "Small Weathers"; *Revel*, "The Middle Voice," "*Oikos*," "Sense of," "Watchers"; *Sierra*, "Island Birds"; *The Southern Review*, "Six Glasses of Water"; *The Yale Review*, "Twilight Sleep."

"Jewelweed" was first published in *A Literary Field Guide to Northern Appalachia*, edited by Todd Davis, Noah Davis, and Carolyn Mahan (University of Georgia Press, 2024); "Mammalian" was first published in *Creature Needs: Writers Respond to the Science of Animal Conservation*, edited by Christopher Kondrich, Lucy Spelman, and Susan Tacent (University of Minnesota Press, 2025). "Six Meditations on a Poem" was first published in *Anne Bradstreet Today*, edited by Mary Eyring and Abram Van Engen (Oxford University Press, 2026).

I am grateful also to Denison University, to the Ohio Arts Council, and to Jill Bialosky for the gift of her belief.

NOTES

In addition to quotations I've attributed directly in my poems, I have echoed or reused phrases and information from other sources, as noted here.

Epigraph: The epigraph to this book comes from Charles Wright's *Littlefoot* (2008).

"Six Notes": John Berryman's "Dream Song 14" from *Collected Poems 1937–1971* (2014).

"Twilight Sleep": Becky Munsterer Sabky's "The Life of a Stranger," *Valley News*; Gholamali Dorooshi's "Catfish Stings: A Report of Two Cases," *Journal of Research in Medical Sciences* (June 2012); Charles Wright's *Littlefoot* (2008).

"Lilac Tree and Lichen": Donald Justice's "*There is a gold light in certain old paintings*" from *Collected Poems* (2004).

"Small Weathers": Tess Gallagher's "Amplitude" from *Amplitude: New and Selected Poems* (1987); W. S. Merwin's "Kore" from *The Compass Flower* (1977); Zach Savich's "My Summer Hospital" from *The Orchard Green and Every Color* (2016); Stanley Plumly's "Dutch Elm" from *Against Sunset* (2016); Jack Gilbert's "A Brief for the Defense" from *Collected Poems* (2012).

"My Documentary Art": Philip Metres's "(More) News from Poems: Investigative / Documentary / Social Poetics on the Tenth Anniversary of the Publication of 'From Reznikoff to Public Enemy.'"

"Mammalian": Tom Harris's "How Bats Work"; Skylar Hopkins et al., "Continued preference for suboptimal habitat reduces bat survival with white-nose syndrome," *Nature Communications*.

"*Oikos*": Horace's *Works and Days* (translated by David W. Tandy and Walter C. Neale, 1997); Thoreau's *Walden* (1854); Issa's "Deep Autumn" from *The Essential Haiku* (translated and edited by Robert Hass, 1994); Virgil's "Fourth Georgic" from *The Georgics of Virgil* (translated by David Ferry, 2005).

"Six Meditations on a Poem": Anne Bradstreet's "The Four Elements" and "For My Dear Son Simon Bradstreet" from *The Works of Anne Bradstreet* (edited by Jeannine Hensley, 2010).

"The Colonists": Lucretius' *On the Nature of the Universe* (translated by Ronald Melville, 1997); "Letters Show How Humans Priced for Sale During Slave Trade," *Washington Informer* (2015).

"Says the Wind": Anton Chekhov's "Who Was to Blame?" from *Selected Stories of Anton Chekhov* (translated by Richard Pevear and Larissa Volokhonsky, 2009).

"The Other Sorrow": Carl Phillips's "Rough Surf in Moonlight" from *Then the War: And Selected Poems, 2007–2020* (2022); Emily Dickinson's letter to Mrs. Jonathan L. Jenkins, late May 1877, from *The Letters of Emily Dickinson* (edited by Cristanne Miller and Domhnall Mitchell, 2024).

"The Bay": James Longenbach's "In the Village" from *Forever* (2021); Stanley Plumly's "Cancer" from *Orphan Hours* (2012).

"Sailing Stones": Kathryn Scanlan's *Aug 9—Fog* (2019).